To

_____

From

_____

Date

_____

Summerside Press™
Minneapolis 55378
www.summersidepress.com

60 Promises to Pray Over Your Children
© 2012 Roy Lessin

ISBN 978-1-60936-197-6

Cover design by Koechel Peterson & Associates
Interior design and typesetting by Jeff Jansen | AestheticSoup.net

Summerside Press™ is an inspirational publisher offering fresh, irresistible books to uplift the heart and engage the mind.

Printed in China.

Promises
to Pray
over your children

Roy Lessin

summerside
PRESS™

Dedicated to my father,
Joseph Aaron Lessin,
who faithfully prayed for me
for more than forty-five years,
and who left me a
spiritual heritage for which
I am eternally grateful.

Contents

Section
1

The Privilege of Blessing

*[Jesus] took the children in
his arms and placed his hands
on their heads and blessed them.*

Mark 10:16 NLT

God loves to bless the lives of children. As parents we have the awesome privilege of extending the blessing of God to each child. Our words can speak the blessing of God, our hands can impart the blessing of God, our hearts can express the blessing of God. As we ask God to bless our children, we are asking for His best, His highest, and His greatest good for their lives.

Children grow and thrive under the blessing of God. As we bless them, our children will hear words of hope, encouragement, and support. Prayers of blessing will not beat them down, but build them up; will not hurt them, but heal them; will not weaken them, but strengthen them; will not lead them astray, but help them follow the good that God has for their lives.

Blessed by the Lord

For as the days of a tree, so shall be the days of My people, and My chosen and elect shall long make use of and enjoy the work of their hands. They shall not labor in vain or bring forth [children] for sudden terror or calamity; for they shall be the descendants of the blessed of the Lord, and their offspring with them.

ISAIAH 65:22–23 AMP

I will remember that when I give Him my heart, God chooses to live within me—body and soul. He fills all of the empty places, His very Spirit inside of me.

ANONYMOUS

Lord, by Your grace, Your power, and Your love, You have lifted the clouds of doom from our household. Thank You for the promise that my children do not face a hopeless, worthless, or meaningless future. You have assured me that my children have not been brought into this world for destruction, but for redemption; not for panic, but for peace; not for emptiness, but completeness; not for frustration, but for the glorification of Your name. Thank You for the promise that my children are "blessed by the Lord."

Because we belong to You, You have saved us from emptiness—from a life of empty words, empty promises, empty desires, empty thoughts, empty goals, empty work, and empty choices. Thank You for freeing us, as a family, from empty relationships with each other.

Thank You, Father, for the blessings You have extended to my family. My children will never face a moment in life when it is not true that they are blessed of the Lord. I pray that regardless of their circumstances, You will help them to always recognize and understand how blessed they are. And for all these blessings, I thank You.

Blessing and Gratitude

Behold, children are a heritage from the Lord, the fruit of the womb a reward. As arrows are in the hand of a warrior, so are the children of one's youth. Happy, blessed, and fortunate is the man whose quiver is filled with them! They will not be put to shame when they speak with their adversaries [in gatherings] at the [city's] gate.

PSALM 127:3–5 AMP

Every material goal, even if it is met, will pass away. But the heritage of children is timeless. Our children are our messages to the future.

BILLY GRAHAM

Heavenly Father, my prayer to You today is one of thanksgiving, gratitude, and praise. Thank You so much for Your favor and marvelous generosity to my family and me. Every good and perfect gift truly comes directly from Your hand to us through Your giving heart of kindness and love.

I cannot begin to express to You how greatly blessed and grateful I am for the gift of my children. I do, with all my heart, receive each life that has come into our family as Your beautiful gift. I cannot find the words to thank You enough.

My children are a testimony of Your grace, a proclamation of Your wisdom, a revelation of Your workmanship, a demonstration of the creative work of Your hands. Thank You that You have given them to me as Your heritage—to know, to enjoy, to love, to care for, to celebrate, to delight in, and to raise so that they too may know You as the greatest heritage of all.

Your Hand Upon Them

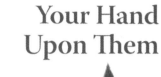

Then they brought little children to Him, that He might touch them; but the disciples rebuked those who brought them. But when Jesus saw it, He was greatly displeased and said to them, "Let the little children come to Me, and do not forbid them; for of such is the kingdom of God."

MARK 10:13–14 NKJV

The heavenly Father welcomes us with open arms and imparts to us blessing upon blessing, not because we are upright but because Jesus Christ has clothed us with His own virtue.

SHERWOOD ELIOT WIRT

Jesus, thank You that I have the wonderful privilege of bringing my children to You in prayer. It means so much to know that each child means so much to You and that You listen to my prayers. Thank You that You do not push my children away from You or keep them at a distance. I am so grateful that You welcome them with outstretched arms; that You embrace them with a full heart of compassion; that You receive them and draw them close to You.

Place Your hand upon my children's heads. I ask that You would bless them with the richest blessings of Your hidden treasures. Touch their lives, Jesus, warm their hearts, fill their cups, make them whole, keep them strong. Teach them Your ways and reveal to them the greatness of Your kingdom, the meekness of Your Spirit, and the beauty of Your ways. May they learn to come to You with every need they have and receive from You every provision that You alone can give.

Spiritual Blessings

Grace to you and peace from God our Father and the Lord Jesus Christ. Blessed be the God and Father of our Lord Jesus Christ, who has blessed us with every spiritual blessing in the heavenly places in Christ, just as He chose us in Him before the foundation of the world, that we should be holy and without blame before Him in love.

EPHESIANS 1:2–4 NKJV

It isn't raining rain for you. It's raining blessing. For, if you will but believe your Father's Word, under that beating rain are springing up spiritual flowers.

J. M. McC

Father, how gracious You are; how blessed I am; how rich is my portion; how full is my cup! You are the perfect Father—loving, caring, providing, giving, sheltering—making a safe place, a restful place, a thriving place for my children and me to come to and abide in. Thank You that the best place, the highest place, and the securest place for us to be is in Jesus Christ.

Bless my children with every spiritual blessing that You have made available through a relationship with Your Son. May Your life be in them, may Your hand be on them, may Your favor be with them. Work in them and through them.

Give them quiet hearts that trust in You; humble hearts that depend on You; grateful hearts that receive from You; joyful hearts that worship You; true hearts that honor You; giving hearts that express You; pure hearts that glorify You; obedient hearts that please You.

Supply Their Needs

My God will liberally supply (fill to the full) your every need according to His riches in glory in Christ Jesus. To our God and Father be glory forever and ever (through the endless eternities of the eternities). Amen.

<small>PHILIPPIANS 4:19–20 AMP</small>

The "air" which our souls need also envelops all of us at all times and on all sides. God is round about us in Christ on every hand, with many-sided and all-sufficient grace. All we need to do is to open our hearts.

<small>OLE HALLESBY</small>

Jesus, You are so wonderful! You are the One the Father has sent for us, sent to us, sent with us, sent in us. May the hearts of my children be taken up with You. May You be their daily song, their constant peace, their abundant joy. May You be their reason to live.

May my children always know how great and abundant is Your supply. I thank You that they are given the lavish riches of Your grace. May they always be quick to come to You, trust in You, and receive from You.

Jesus, assure them that they will never meet a fear You have not conquered; that they will never face an enemy You have not defeated; that they will never have a need You cannot meet; that they will never face a temptation You have not overcome; that they will never have a burden You cannot lift; that they will never face a problem You have not solved; that they will never have a bondage You cannot break; that they will never experience a moment when You do not care. Thank You for being all they need.

His Goodness

Know that the LORD, He is God; it is He who has made us, and not we ourselves; we are His people and the sheep of His pasture. Enter into His gates with thanksgiving, and into His courts with praise. Be thankful to Him, and bless His name. For the LORD is good; His mercy is everlasting, and His truth endures to all generations.

PSALM 100:3–5 NKJV

*T*he God who made your children will hear your petitions. He has promised to do so. After all, He loves them more than you do.

DR. JAMES DOBSON

Thank You, heavenly Father, for being a good God and doing good things for us, to us, and in us. I thank You that You are good to my children and Your eye is on every detail of their lives.

Thank You that no one can ever be as good to them as You are! Keep my children in the center of Your love and Your designed purpose, assuring them that You are working all things together for the good, and fitting them into Your good plan for their lives.

May the goodness of Your light shine on them; may the goodness of Your grace be with them; may the goodness of Your love be in them. Through Your goodness give them: the hugs of Your mercies; the warmth of Your nearness; the delights of Your fellowship; the joys of Your friendship; the peace of Your presence; the rest of Your comfort; the favor of Your smile.

The Blessing of the Lord

And the Lord spoke to Moses, saying: "Speak to Aaron and his sons, saying, 'This is the way you shall bless the children of Israel. Say to them: "The Lord bless you and keep you; the Lord make His face shine upon you, and be gracious to you; the Lord lift up His countenance upon you, and give you peace."' So they shall put My name on the children of Israel, and I will bless them."

Numbers 6:22–27 nkjv

There are two requirements for our proper enjoyment of every earthly blessing which God bestows on us—a thankful reflection on the goodness of the Giver and a deep sense of the unworthiness of the receiver. The first would make us grateful, the second humble.

Hannah More

Father, my heart is full of praise and gratitude to You for blessing me with the gift of my beautiful children. I want to say, over and over again, "Thank You so much!" Your blessings leave me in awe. You have enriched their lives in more ways than I could ever imagine.

Your blessing, Father, means everything. My prayer and deep desire is that my children will be blessed of the Lord. May Your blessing be upon them. As Aaron spoke Your blessing over the people of Israel, so I speak Your blessing over my children today.

Father, bless them with Your favor and kindness; keep them by Your power and strength; deliver them from all evil. May Your face shine upon them with the light of Your radiant love; may they know the abundant riches of Your amazing grace; bestow upon them the smile of Your countenance; shield their hearts and minds with Your abiding peace—the perfect peace that passes all understanding. Amen!

Section 2

The Comfort of Protection

This I declare about the LORD: He alone is my refuge, my place of safety; he is my God, and I trust him. He will cover you with his feathers.... He will shelter you with his wings. His faithful promises are your armor and protection.

PSALM 91:2, 4 NLT

It's important for children to feel safe and secure. Many things can trouble them and cause them to become frightened and insecure—a dark room, a loud noise, unfamiliar surroundings, a strange face, a storm. The need to be sheltered, protected, and cared for remain with them throughout life.

When the disciples were with Jesus on a stormy sea, they became fearful and came to Him for help (He was asleep on the boat at the time). It took Jesus but a moment to quiet the storm and calm their fears. They needed to be reassured they were in the presence of the One who cared about them and could protect them from any storm.

Through prayer, we can ask that our children be daily reassured of God's presence, His watchful care, His hand of covering, and His ever-present help in every time of need.

Pour Out Your Spirit

The LORD who made you and helps you says: Do not be afraid, O Jacob, my servant, O dear Israel, my chosen one. For I will pour out water to quench your thirst and to irrigate your parched fields. And I will pour out my Spirit on your descendants, and my blessing on your children. They will thrive like watered grass, like willows on a riverbank.

ISAIAH 44:2–4 NLT

For [God] is, indeed, a wonderful Father who longs to pour out His mercy upon us, and whose majesty is so great that He can transform us from deep within.

ST. TERESA OF AVILA

My Father, what a wonderful God You are. You have promised to pour out Your Spirit on my children. Pour over them Your abundant mercies, Your abundant grace, Your abundant goodness, Your abundant blessings, Your abundant love. May they always drink from Your fountain of joy; wash in the river of Your mercies; be touched by Your refreshing rains. Quench their thirsty souls, water the garden of their hearts, and keep their spirits in Your healing streams. Cause them to thrive, flourish, and prosper in life and in their relationship with You.

My children are handmade by You. You are their designer. You are their helper and keeper. I ask that they will never doubt, question, or wonder who they are, where they came from, or where they are going. May they live free of fear—safe from its bondage, kept from its paralyzing grip, protected from everything that would terrify and hinder them from experiencing all that You have for them. May their hearts be full of expectancy and assurance, knowing that You have set them free.

Stay Strong

Give all your worries and cares to God, for he cares about you. Stay alert! Watch out for your great enemy, the devil. He prowls around like a roaring lion, looking for someone to devour. Stand firm against him, and be strong in your faith. Remember that your Christian brothers and sisters all over the world are going through the same kind of suffering you are.

1 Peter 5:7–9 NLT

Prayer is a powerful thing, for God has bound and tied himself thereto. None can believe how powerful prayer is, and what it is able to effect, but those who have learned it by experience.

Martin Luther

Lord, according to Your Word my children have an Enemy who wants to rob, kill, and destroy their faith and trust in You. I thank You for helping them stand firm, for doing in their lives what is more powerful than what the Enemy seeks to do. You are greater than anything or anyone who would come against them. Help them to remember that and to draw strength from it.

Father, may Your truth always keep them from his lies. May Your light always keep them from his darkness; Your wisdom always keep them from his confusion; Your peace always keep them from his restlessness; Your pathway always keep them from his dead-end road.

Give each child the grace to cast all their worries and cares on You. Protect them from being weighed down with concerns that You never intended them to carry. Help them, by Your grace, to stand firm against every scheme of the Devil, to be strong, and to daily grow in their faith and confidence in You. Help them to pray for and love others with a sincere heart of understanding and love.

Daily Bread

Your words were found, and I ate them, and Your word was to me the joy and rejoicing of my heart; For I am called by Your name, O LORD God of hosts.

JEREMIAH 15:16 NKJV

Part of our job is to expect that, if we are attentive and willing, God will "give us prayer," will give us the things we need, "our daily bread," to heal and grow in love.

ROBERTA BONDI

Gracious Father, I ask that my children will always hunger after Your words. Increase their appetite. May they find Your words to be delightful, whole and pure, abundant in grace, rich in mercy. Feed them, Father, with fresh bread, living bread, daily bread. Nurture them in their spirits, teach them that they cannot live on bread alone, and that they need You to sustain them with every word that comes from Your mouth. Break to them the bread of life.

Thank You, Father, that Your words can be found, can be eaten, and can be known. May my children find Your words to be the joy and delight of their hearts. May they daily realize the awesome privilege they have to be called by Your name, to be a part of a forever family, and to receive the words spoken to them by their heavenly Father.

Thank You that we can know Your heart. Thank You that we can hear Your heart through the words You have spoken. Your words are like none other—their taste is sweet, their sound is a symphony, their power is a transforming light. They are a lamp to our feet and a light to our pathway.

Be Content

Let your conduct be without covetousness; be content with such things as you have. For He Himself has said, "I will never leave you nor forsake you." So we may boldly say: "The LORD is my helper; I will not fear. What can man do to me?"

HEBREWS 13:5–6 NKJV

Contentment is never a matter of circumstances; contentment is always a state of communion—a daily embracing of God. A thankfulness for all the gifts—and moments and life, just as He gives it.

ANN VOSKAMP

I thank You, Gracious Father, that my children can live with contentment in their hearts. Help them to be content when they have much and when they have little. May they never lose the attitude of gratefulness. May thanksgiving always be on their lips. Help them to understand that the addition of things will not increase their joy, and the absence of things will not diminish their joy.

Give them, Father, their daily bread. Bless them with simple pleasures, with rich relationships, with heartfelt joys, with fruit for their labors, with strength for their days. Assure them in a thousand different ways that You are their helper, and they do not need to fear.

Thank You for the wonderful ways You take care of my family. Thank You for the peace we have in knowing that even though our circumstances change, You never change. You are never inconsistent, You are never undecided, You are never unsure about what You should do, and You are never limited in what You can do. Thank You that Your resources can never be depleted.

Shield of Protection

But You, O Lord, are a shield for me, my glory, and the lifter of my head. With my voice I cry to the Lord, and He hears and answers me out of His holy hill.... I lay down and slept; I wakened again, for the Lord sustains me.

PSALM 3:3–5 AMP

Incredible as it may seem, God wants our companionship. He wants to have us close to Him. He wants to be a father to us, to shield us, to protect us, to counsel us, and to guide us in our way through life.

BILLY GRAHAM

Thank You, Lord, that You are our hiding place, our safe place, our shielded place. Thank You that You are the defender and the protector of my children. I pray for their safety today, for the ministry of Your protective angels to be around them.

May Your encouragement be with them, Your hope be in them, and Your grace be upon them. If they are burdened, lighten their load; if they are troubled, calm their storm; if they are discouraged, lift their spirits; if they are unsure, strengthen their faith; if they are weary, renew their strength; if they are perplexed, guide their way; if they are unsteady, be their rock; if they are tempted, make a way of escape; if they lack understanding, be their wisdom; if they doubt love, reveal Your heart.

Thank You so much, that when we come to You and cry out to You, we can know with all certainty that You hear our words, You know our heart, and You answer prayer.

Peaceful Covenant

Now may the God of peace who brought up our Lord Jesus from the dead, that great Shepherd of the sheep, through the blood of the everlasting covenant, make you complete in every good work to do His will, working in you what is well pleasing in His sight, through Jesus Christ, to whom be glory forever and ever. Amen.

HEBREWS 13:20–21 NKJV

God is the shepherd in search of His lamb. His legs are scratched, His feet are sore and His eyes are burning. He scales the cliffs and traverses the fields.... He cups His hands to His mouth and calls into the canyon. And the name He calls is yours.

MAX LUCADO

Lord, today I pray in agreement with the prayer written in Hebrews 13:20–21. I ask that it will be specifically answered in the lives of my children. I pray that the perfect peace that only comes from You will guard the hearts and minds of each child. I thank You that Jesus is their Shepherd and my children are Your sheep. Thank You for feeding them when they are hungry; restoring them when they wander; defending them when they are under attack. Thank You for being their door into Your green pastures.

Thank You, Lord, for Your shed blood and Your covenant promises. Thank You for all that Your shed blood has provided and purchased. May my children overcome the Enemy through the blood of the Lamb, and may Your blood cleanse them from all sin.

Work within my children Your will, Your good work, and all that is well pleasing in Your sight. Bless them today through Jesus Christ. To You, Lord, be all the glory forever and ever. Amen.

Sun and Shield

For the LORD God is a sun and shield; the LORD bestows favor and honor; no good thing does he withhold from those whose walk is blameless.

PSALM 84:11 NIV

God longs to give favor—that is, spiritual strength and health—to those who seek Him, and Him alone. He grants spiritual favors and victories, not because the one who seeks him is holier than anyone else, but in order to make His holy beauty and His great redeeming power known.

ST. TERESA OF AVILA

Heavenly Father, thank You for being so kind, so gracious, and so generous. Thank You that You give, and give, and give again. Thank You that Your generosity is extended to us through Your abundant grace and favor.

As the sun rises in the east, may the light of Your love also greet my children each morning. I pray that the brilliance of Your light will shine on their lives, and that they will see You as the sunshine of each day.

May You be the Shield that is about them, keeping them safe from every foe that wants to steal their peace, rob them of their joy, and keep them from Your blessings. I pray against every lie that would try to persuade them that You can't be trusted.

I ask that their hearts will rest in Your care. May they be fully persuaded that You will not hold back anything from them that is good and right for them to have. May they be faithful to take care of the things that concern You, knowing that You will be faithful to take care of the things that concern them.

Section 3

The Beauty of Character

Let the beauty of the LORD
our God be upon us.

PSALM 90:17 KJV

Like clay, our lives need to be formed, molded, and shaped into the image of the One who created us. Godly character is not a gift that we instantly receive, but is something that is formed within us by placing our lives in God's hands, receiving His grace, depending on His Spirit, and choosing to do what is pleasing in His sight.

It is important for parents to pray that our children will not only know the Lord and follow the Lord, but that they will also yield to the Lord so that His character can be formed within them. No life is more beautiful than the one whose heart is filled with loveliness, whose attitudes are filled with kindness, whose words are spoken with gentleness, and whose behavior is marked by righteousness.

Learn to Fear God

Call them all together—men, women, children, and the foreigners living in your towns—so they may hear this Book of Instruction and learn to fear the LORD your God and carefully obey all the terms of these instructions. Do this so that your children who have not known these instructions will hear them and will learn to fear the LORD your God.

DEUTERONOMY 31:12–13 NLT

The fear of the Lord doesn't make you timid. It doesn't make you weak. The fear of the Lord gives you strength. When you fear the Lord you don't have to fear anything else.

DEREK PRINCE

Lord, to fear You is a good thing. You have said that to fear You with reverential awe is the beginning of wisdom and moves us away from evil. I pray that the fear of the Lord will be established deep within the hearts of my children. Help them to daily stand in the light of Your holiness with a broken and contrite heart; to bow before You with a meek and quiet spirit; to kneel at Your feet in quiet worship as they behold Your glory and Your majesty.

I pray that as they fear You they would always run toward You and never run away from You. Let them always understand that to fear You means they would never desire to do anything to grieve or sadden Your heart. May each child live to be a God-pleaser and to bring a smile to Your face. May they always care about what You think and how You feel.

As You bless them, Lord, I pray that they will daily be a blessing to You.

An Honorable Life

Honor your father and your mother, that your days may be long upon the land which the LORD your God is giving you.

EXODUS 20:12 NKJV

It is good to be with Jesus and to remain here forever. What greater happiness or higher honor could we have than to be with God, to be made like Him, and to live in His light?

ST. ANASTASIUS OF SINAI

Jesus, as I pray for my children, I am reminded of the importance of living an honorable life and of giving honor to whom honor is due. Give my children sensitive and caring hearts for others that will bring honor to others. Help them be honorable in their actions and attitudes and be generously responsive to the needs of others. May they, in their submission to You, be careful to show respect to those who have been placed over them.

May they be wise students, productive workers, good citizens, supportive team members, and respected companions. Help them know how to follow so that they will learn how to lead; help them know how to give so that they will know how to prosper; help them know how to bend so that they can stand tall.

Teach them to walk as You walked and to honor their Father in heaven as You honored Him when You walked on the earth. May their days be long, may their hearts be full, may their lives be enriched, and may their blessings be abundant.

Clothed with Humility

You younger men, likewise, be subject to your elders; and all of you, clothe yourselves with humility toward one another, for God is opposed to the proud, but gives grace to the humble. Humble yourselves, therefore, under the mighty hand of God, that He may exalt you at the proper time.

1 PETER 5:5–6 NASB

Bless every humble soul who, in these days of stress and strain, preaches sermons without words.

PETER MARSHALL

God, may the hearts of my children never be filled with pride, be puffed up, or look down on others. May they be humble vessels who are aware of their needs, who are broken and contrite before You, and who realize, moment by moment, their total dependence on Your grace.

I pray that my children will honor those whom You have placed over them, that they will show respect and give honor to everyone, especially to the elderly, and that they will learn to reflect Your heart when You said, "I have not come to be served but to serve."

Thank You that You are their all-in-all, that You are above all, and that You rule over all that is in heaven and on earth. Thank You for those You place over my children's lives. Thank You for using those people to shape them, mold their character, conform them to Your image, and help prepare them for the things You have prepared for them.

Biblical Encouragement

Therefore, since we are surrounded by such a huge crowd of witnesses to the life of faith, let us strip off every weight that slows us down, especially the sin that so easily trips us up. And let us run with endurance the race God has set before us.

HEBREWS 12:1 NLT

If our children have the background of a godly, happy home and this unshakable faith that the Bible is indeed the Word of God, they will have a foundation that the forces of hell cannot shake.

RUTH BELL GRAHAM

Thank You, Lord, for the example of the men and women of faith who have followed You through life's journey. Thank You for the testimonies of their trust, the fruit of their faithfulness, and the witness of their walk. I pray that what has been written about them in Your Word will be a source of encouragement to my children, and that their patience and endurance would encourage my children to wait on You in full assurance of faith.

Bless my children with the blessings of Abraham. Help them to learn from Daniel to be uncompromising; from Joseph to do what is right by not sinning against You; from Gideon to be strong and courageous; from Moses to hear Your voice and have Your glory shine upon their faces; from Ruth to fully indentify with You and Your people; from Sarah to believe that You can do the impossible; from Samuel to recognize Your voice and speak out Your words; from David to be a person after Your own heart. Use them to be a blessing, an encouragement, and an example to others of what it means to follow You.

Enduring Character

We can rejoice, too, when we run into problems and trials, for we know that they help us develop endurance. And endurance develops strength of character, and character strengthens our confident hope of salvation. And this hope will not lead to disappointment. For we know how dearly God loves us.

ROMANS 5:3–5 NLT

God, the master artist, is most concerned about expressing himself—His thoughts and His intentions—through what He paints in our character.... [He] wants to paint a beautiful portrait of His Son in and through your life.

JONI EARECKSON TADA

Father, keep the hearts of my children close to You; keep their thoughts fixed on You; keep their spirits strong in You. May Your grace draw them to Your heart, Your will, Your love—moment by moment, day after day. In times of difficulty or trials help them to lean upon You and draw their strength from You. Give them the endurance they need to stand firm, to continue on, to press in, and to press through everything and anything that seeks to hinder them or sidetrack them from following Your plan and doing Your will.

May they always have keen vision to watch out for the attacks from the Devil—to resist his temptations; to reject his lies; to refuse his condemnation; to reject his accusations. Build their characters. Lead them away from disappointment.

I pray that when they are carrying burdens, they would learn to cast them on You; when they are anxious, they would depend on Your promises; when they become discouraged, their hope would be renewed. Assure them today, Father, how dearly You love them.

Kingdom Power

For the kingdom of God is not in word but in power.

1 CORINTHIANS 4:20 NKJV

Let there be no limit to what we take to God in prayer, so that there may be no limit to God's reign and rule in all of life.

ROGER HAZELTON

Thank You, God, for the power of Your kingdom—the power to change, to transform, to turn things upside down for the good, the power to make all things new in our hearts and lives. Thank You that Your ways are higher than our ways; Your plans are better than our plans; Your wisdom is greater than our wisdom.

I pray that my children will always see life in the light and understanding of how You see things. May their eyes behold You and may they never forget what You show them. May they know Your mind and think Your thoughts. Teach them, Father, the ways of Your kingdom—the way of losing to gain, of dying to live, of becoming weak to find Your strength, of possessing nothing yet making others rich, of taking the lowly place in order to be lifted up, of forsaking what is temporary in order to inherit the things that will last forever.

May the power of Christ rest on them and may His kingdom reign within them. Move them from anything that is superficial to what is genuine, from what is false to what is true, from what is empty to what is abundant, from what is meaningless to what is of eternal worth.

Section
4

The Joys of Community

Through love serve one another.

GALATIANS 5:13 NKJV

God has not only called us to know and enjoy Him, but He has also called us to know and enjoy others. Each child of God has been placed into a family of believers. The outflow of our fellowship with God will bring us into fellowship with others. God has made us dependent on one another. We need others and others need us to grow, to be supported, to be helped, to be encouraged, to be loved, to be prayed for, to be enriched, to be guided, to be cared for, and to be blessed.

As children grow and mature, we parents need to be in prayer about the friendships our children form and the influence their lives will have on others. Through every stage of life, children can be a blessing to those around them, including family members, classmates, teachers, and others in the community.

From Generation to Generation

I will establish My covenant between Me and you and your descendants after you throughout their generations for an everlasting, solemn pledge, to be a God to you and to your posterity after you... and I will be their God.

Genesis 17:7–8 AMP

The God to whom you commit yourself and everything that concerns you is huge.... He is the One who sees. He is the One who knows. He is the One who acts on behalf of His children.

Beth Moore

Father, according to Your covenant promise to Abraham to always be our God and the God of our children, please reveal Yourself to the hearts of my children and fulfill Your covenant promises to them.

You are the God who is faithful to every generation that loves and puts its trust in You. Thank You for showing Your faithfulness to generations past in countless ways and at countless times, for showing Your faithfulness to my generation and me, and for showing Yourself faithful to the generations to come.

I put my complete trust in You. You have promised to be the God of my children at all times and in all ways. Be their God in their going out and coming in, in their choices and decisions, in their waiting times and busy times, in their happy times and times of sorrow, in their times of testing and their times of celebration. Because You will always be their God, I know they will always have all they need. Thank You for fulfilling Your promises to my children.

Godly Relationships

Do not be so deceived and misled! Evil companionships (communion, associations) corrupt and deprave good manners and morals and character.

1 Corinthians 15:33 AMP

A single good friend is a treasure worth more than gold or precious stones. Money can buy many things, good and evil. All the wealth of the world could not buy you a friend or pay you for the loss of one.

C. D. Prentice

Heavenly Father, thank You for the truth and light we receive from Your Word. Thank You that Your wisdom can keep us from going through heartaches and sorrows that You never intended for us to know in our experience. Protect my children from being influenced by evil companionships.

I pray that my children will learn to trust in Your Word for each decision they make, will know beyond a doubt that Your ways are the best, will be assured that You will not withhold anything from them that is good, and will have the peace and satisfaction of knowing that their obedience to You means living without regrets.

Also please bless my children in their relationships throughout their lives. Guard them from being deceived or misled by others. May they know what it means to be a good friend, and may they always be blessed with good friends—those who are growing in faith, strong in character, upright in conduct, loyal and supportive, true and trusting, helpful and kind.

Fulfilled Promises

For the promise [of the Holy Spirit] is to and for you and your children, and to and for all that are far away, [even] to and for as many as the Lord our God invites and bids to come to Himself.

ACTS 2:39 AMP

We have ample evidence that the Lord is able to guide. The promises cover every imaginable situation. All we need to do is to take the hand He stretches out.

JIM ELLIOT

Thank You, God, that Your promises are not just for generations past, but are for my generation and for my children's generation. Thank You that what You promised the early church, You have also promised us. Assure my children's hearts that You are not only the promise keeper of the past, but also the promise keeper of today and the promise keeper of their futures.

You give them promises to trust in, and You fulfill them in Your time. You are a promise maker and a promise keeper. Thank You that Your timing is always perfect, that You are never too late, that You never make a promise that is empty, and that You never forget a promise that You have made.

God, Your promises to my children are the divine assurances of Your will. Thank You. Fulfill in them the promise of the fullness of Your Spirit, the promise of Your call upon their lives, and the promise of Your presence with them always.

Leave a Legacy

Blessings crown the head of the righteous.... The memory of the righteous will be a blessing.

PROVERBS 10:6–7 NIV

Notice words of compassion. Seek out deeds of kindness. These are like the doves from heaven, pointing out to you who are the ones blessed with inner grace and beauty.

CHRISTOPHER DE VINCK

Father, thank You that You bless our lives so that we can be a blessing to others. Truly, Father, Your blessings upon us are more precious than the royal crowns that are worn upon the heads of the kings and queens of this world. I pray that by Your grace and power You will stir within my children the things that will help them to bring encouragement and enrichment to the lives of those they touch.

Give to them the soothing words that will heal a hurting heart; the wise words that will guide a seeking heart; the assuring words that will comfort a grieving heart; the accepting words that will embrace a lonely heart; the affirming words that will strengthen a fearful heart; the life-giving words that will fill an empty heart.

I pray that through the testimony of the lives of my children there will be others who know You better and love You more. May there be many who will say of them, "I thank God for you." I ask that through their choices, their faith, and their obedience to Your will, my children will leave a legacy that will impact their generation and generations to come.

Know Love

Beloved, let us love one another, for love is of God; and everyone who loves is born of God and knows God. He who does not love does not know God, for God is love.... And we have known and believed the love that God has for us. God is love, and he who abides in love abides in God, and God in him.

1 JOHN 4:7–8, 16 NKJV

Because of His boundless love, He became what we are in order that He might make us what He is.

ST. IRENAEUS

God, I pray that Your love will be poured into the lives of my children and that they will know the meaning of love at its deepest level. I pray that they will be lovers of God and that through them others will know Your love. Flood their hearts, fill their minds, move their wills, form their words, motivate their actions, and shape their character with Your love. May they speak the truth in love, walk in love, and abide in love.

Thank You, God, that You are love and all that love means. To know You is to know love, to receive You is to receive love, to have You is to have love, to express You is to express love. Thank You that Your love will never wear out, fade out, burn out, or tire out.

I pray that my children will know the freedom that love brings to their lives. May they come to know for themselves, and extend to others, Your unconditional love—without partiality, without limitations, without measure.

Section 5

The Proclamation of Praise

Let everything that has breath
praise the LORD. Praise the LORD.
PSALM 150:6 NKJV

We were made to celebrate, to be filled with gladness, and to have our hearts overflow with joy. Praise should always be on our lips and thanksgiving in our hearts. We were made to have God be the center of our joy and the focus of our praise. It is from Him, to Him, and through Him that our voices can rejoice, that our mouths can be filled with laughter, and that our hearts can find, at His right hand, the pleasures that are ours forevermore.

We must pray that our children will have happy dispositions, that they will live contented lives, that they will sing new songs to the Lord, that their cups will be full and running over, that they will be worshipers of God in spirit and truth, and that they will always carry a melody of praise in their hearts.

Praise the Name of the Lord

Young men and young women, old men and children. Let them all praise the name of the LORD. For his name is very great; his glory towers over the earth and heaven! He has made his people strong, honoring his faithful ones.

PSALM 148:12–14 NLT

It is right and good that we, for all things, at all times, and in all places, give thanks and praise to You, O God. We worship You, we confess to You, we praise You, we bless You, we sing to You, and we give thanks to You: Maker, Nourisher, Guardian, Healer, Lord, and Father of all.

LANCELOT ANDREWES

Father, may my children always carry Your praise in their hearts. Keep their eyes open to see You, their ears open to hear You, and their hearts open to love You. May they taste and see that You are good. May they touch You with the hand of faith and know the reality of Your presence. May their days be full of joy and may their lives be daily blessed. Thank You for Your promise to keep them.

I ask that they will know, more and more, how great You are, how glorious are Your ways, how awesome are Your works. May they sing Your songs of joy. May they speak Your words of life. May they sound forth Your praises. May worship fill their spirits, truth fill their minds, and wisdom fill their understanding. Bring constant gratitude and thankfulness to their tongues.

Lord, keep them strong in Your strength, blessed with Your blessings, full in Your abundance. Keep their faith ever growing, ever reaching for more of what You have for them as they see Your faithfulness revealed to them day by day.

Perfect Praise

And they said to Him, Do You hear what these are saying? And Jesus replied to them, Yes; have you never read, Out of the mouths of babes and unweaned infants You have made (provided) perfect praise?

MATTHEW 21:16 AMP

Let us give all that lies within us...to pure praise, to pure loving adoration, and to worship from a grateful heart—a heart that is trained to look up.

AMY CARMICHAEL

Father in heaven, holy is Your name. I ask that my children will worship You in spirit and in truth. I pray they will see Your glory, sit at Your feet, behold Your face, and be overcome by Your beauty. May Your praise daily be on their lips.

May they never lose the awe that comes from fixing their gaze on You. May they worship You with the music of praise, with the words of gratitude, with the actions of love, with the attitudes of righteousness, with the shouts of joy, and with the new songs of the Spirit that are born out of a deep devotion to You.

May their lives be a daily celebration. Help them to continually drink from the river of Your mercies, break bread at Your table, and delight themselves in the pleasures of Your companionship. May they always walk in Your freshest footsteps, in newness of life, in fellowship with Your people, and in the joy of their salvation. Thank You that all You are is available to my children and me through all our days.

Let Us Worship

The sea is his, and he made it: and his hands formed the dry land. O come, let us worship and bow down: let us kneel before the LORD our maker. For he is our God; and we are the people of his pasture, and the sheep of his hand.

PSALM 95:5–7 KJV

Our God is so wonderfully good, and lovely, and blessed in every way that the mere fact of belonging to Him is enough for an untellable fullness of joy!

HANNAH WHITALL SMITH

Lord, I worship You. You are wonderful and all that You do is marvelous. You are beyond description, and Your ways are past finding out. Your riches never tarnish, Your glory never grows dim, Your wonders never cease, Your beauty never fades, Your power never weakens, Your love never ends. Thank You for being our God and allowing us to be Your people. Thank You for the beauty of the relationship we can experience with You.

I pray that my children will be worshipers of You in spirit and in truth. May their hearts be caught up in Your majesty. May their meditation be sweet. Each day, may they discover something new about the breadth, the length, the height, and the depth of Your boundless love.

May their spirits find a resting place at Your altar; may their knees bend before You in true devotion; may their souls find the pleasures that await them at Your right hand; may their hearts discover what it means to have fullness of joy.

High Praise

I will extol You, my God, O King; and I will bless Your name forever and ever [with grateful, affectionate praise]. Every day [with its new reasons] will I bless You [affectionately and gratefully praise You]; yes, I will praise Your name forever and ever. Great is the Lord and highly to be praised; and His greatness is [so vast and deep as to be] unsearchable.

<small>PSALM 145:1–3 AMP</small>

We can go through all the activities of our days in joyful awareness of God's presence with whispered prayers of praise and adoration flowing continuously from our hearts.

<small>RICHARD J. FOSTER</small>

Lord, You are great! I pray that the eyes of my children will remain wide open to see Your awesome-ness. May they know how vast is Your greatness, how deep is Your love, how high are Your ways, how rich are Your treasures, how abundant are Your blessings, how full are Your joys, how generous are Your gifts.

May my children never think that You are too small, that Your presence is distant, that Your power is limited, that Your love is conditional, that Your help is unavailable, that Your grace is insufficient. In their inadequacies and human limitations may they learn to say, "I can do all things—big things, little things, unpleasant things, hard things, inconvenient things—through Christ who strengthens me" (Philippians 4:13).

Thank You, Lord, that no matter how much we know of You, there is more to learn; no matter how much You have given us, there is more to receive; no matter how much You have shown to us, there is more to behold. We praise Your name.

Living Water

Now on the final and most important day of the Feast, Jesus stood, and He cried in a loud voice, If any man is thirsty, let him come to Me and drink! He who believes in Me [who cleaves to and trusts in and relies on Me] as the Scripture has said, from his innermost being shall flow [continuously] springs and rivers of living water.

JOHN 7:37–38 AMP

From God, great and small, rich and poor, draw living water from a living spring, and those who serve Him freely and gladly will receive grace answering to grace.

THOMAS À KEMPIS

Lord Jesus, the promises You have made to us are truly amazing, awesome, wondrous, and life changing. What joys and wonders are ours when we believe in You and receive from You.

I pray that my children will not miss out on one thing that You desire to give them. May they, in their spiritual thirst, come to You and drink. I pray that in their innermost being will flow the rivers of Your Holy Spirit—rivers of grace, rivers of mercy, rivers of renewal, rivers of refreshing, rivers of healing. May Your life bubble up within them, may Your praises spring up in their hearts, and may Your love flow through them.

I pray that they will abide in the river of Your delights. By faith, may they step into the flow and the freedom that Your Holy Spirit brings. May they walk out to where the water is ankle high, knee high, waist high, chin high, and into the waters they can only swim in.

Praise from the Heart

Stand up and bless the LORD your God forever and ever! Blessed be Your glorious name, which is exalted above all blessing and praise! You alone are the LORD; You have made heaven, the heaven of heavens, with all their host, the earth and everything on it, the seas and all that is in them, and You preserve them all. The host of heaven worships You.

NEHEMIAH 9:5–6 NKJV

Prayer enlarges the heart until it is capable of containing God's gift of Himself. Ask and seek, and your heart will grow big enough to receive Him and keep Him as your own.

MOTHER TERESA

Father, I pray that my children will be worshipers of God. Fill their hearts with hallelujahs. May they sing to You psalms, hymns, and spiritual songs. May their voices be filled with rejoicing, may their tongues proclaim Your praise, may their hearts be filled with thanksgiving. May they walk in the excitement of Your presence, in the wonder of Your works, in the freedom of Your purity, in the greatness of Your power. May they unite with those who declare that You alone are worthy. May You be their daily delight, the joy and the rejoicing of their hearts.

Thank You, Lord, that above all Your blessings, You are the greatest blessing of all; above all Your gifts, You are the greatest gift of all; above all Your joys, You are the greatest joy of all. Higher than what You give, You are the Giver; higher than creation, You are the Creator; higher than health, You are the Healer; higher than redemption, You are the Redeemer. To have You is to have all—the highest, the greatest, the best.

He Hears Us

Now this is the confidence that we have in Him, that if we ask anything according to His will, He hears us. And if we know that He hears us, whatever we ask, we know that we have the petitions that we have asked of Him.

1 JOHN 5:14–15 NKJV

The cross did what man could not do. It granted us the right to talk with, love, and even live with God.

MAX LUCADO

What a glorious privilege You have given to me, Father, to be able to come to You in prayer, to present the needs of my children, to bring to You my requests, and to share my deepest desires for my family. Thank You that I can come to You at anytime, anywhere, with anything I have on my heart and know that You will listen.

Make my children people of prayer. Teach them how to pray, guide them when they pray, and encourage them as they pray. May they learn to come to You, to lean on You, to wait on You, to listen to You, to hear from You, to open their hearts to You, to ask of You, and to receive from You.

Encourage them to knock because the door will be opened; to ask because they will receive; to seek because they will find. May they be free of any doubt or uncertainty regarding Your will. May they pray with full assurance, with boldness, and with the confidence of faith, knowing that You hear their prayers and answer them.

Section
6

The Benefits of Growth

*Grow in the grace and knowledge of our
Lord and Savior Jesus Christ. To Him be
the glory both now and forever. Amen.*

2 PETER 3:18 NKJV

A newborn baby brings a special joy and delight that is beyond what words can express. Yet, no parent desires to see their baby remain a baby and never grow into adulthood. Loving parents seek to train, teach, help, and pray for their children, with the desire to see them grow into responsible and productive adults who will fully and faithfully fulfill the unique plan God has for their lives.

Through prayer, we parents can ask God to plant the eternal seed of His life within the hearts of our children. We can pray that this seed will be watered by His Word and warmed by the sunshine of His presence, love, and care. Prayer can also cover that seed and help protect it so it will become rooted in love, grown in grace, and become a fruitful and flourishing vine within our children's lives.

Peaceful Teacher

All your children shall be taught by the LORD, and great shall be the peace of your children.

ISAIAH 54:13 NKJV

To reach a child's mind a teacher must capture his heart. Only if a child feels right can he think right.

HAIM G. GINOTT

Lord, thank You for covering my children with peace. Please guide and direct them daily, making Your peace their peace. I pray that You will give them peaceful hearts and minds and help them to walk in the ways of peace.

May my children be taught by You—above all voices, may they hear Your voice; above all pathways, may they know Your ways; above all advice, may they learn Your counsel; above all knowledge, may they have Your understanding; above all opinions, may they have Your wisdom.

Lord, let each of my children seek You as their teacher, and may they fully receive Your wisdom. Be their instructor, their guide, their helper. Teach them how to walk with You and learn from You. Open their minds to be teachable and to desire Your wisdom and Your peaceful ways above all. Open their understanding to learn of You, open their eyes to see You, and open their hearts to know and love You.

Spiritual Foundations

Blessed are those who hunger and thirst for righteousness, for they will be filled.

MATTHEW 5:6 NIV

Sometimes remembering the day of our salvation or remembering answered prayer is the last knot on the end of our rope to cling to. ...Looking back at the foundation of our faith is a positive activity.

VIRGINIA THOMSON

Lord, as my children grow, I ask that they will never outgrow their pursuit of Your will, their desire for Your ways, their hunger for Your Word, their dependence on Your strength, and their need for Your grace. May the spiritual foundations that are laid in their hearts when they are young help them as adults to build strong lives of faith and obedience, hope and trust, righteousness and freedom, love and compassion.

May they remember everything You do for them, everything You have provided for them, everything You have taught them, and everything You have done to bless them. I pray that they will never forget who You are and what You have said. Bless them, Lord, with good memories, keen understanding, sweet remembrances, sound minds, and practical understanding.

May we as a family cherish with full hearts all Christ has done for us—shedding His blood, extending forgiveness, providing salvation, and freely giving His love. May we hunger for His righteousness today and all the days of our lives.

Follow Wise Instruction

My child, listen when your father corrects you. Don't neglect your mother's instruction. What you learn from them will crown you with grace and be a chain of honor around your neck.

PROVERBS 1:8–9 NLT

A wise gardener plants his seeds, then has the good sense not to dig them up every few days to see if a crop is on the way. Likewise, we must be patient as God brings the answers...in His own good time.

QUIN SHERRER

Thank You, Lord, for the place You have given me in the lives of my children. I am so grateful that You have ordained for me, by Your grace and Holy Spirit, to speak into their lives through a right example, wise words, loving correction, and practical instruction. Please help me to continue to give loving correction and wise instruction to my children. And grant them the hearts to receive them.

I pray that my children will be wise and continue to grow in wisdom as they hear Your instruction, read Your Word, and learn from the circumstances and relationships You bring into their lives. I pray that they will always be good hearers and listeners of Your voice, and strong followers of Your will. Help them to see life from Your point of view and as they make choices, to always live with the values of eternity before them.

I ask that they will treasure Your truth in their hearts and seek out Your approval. May they live each day with the crown of Your grace upon their heads and the chain of Your honor and favor around their necks.

Grow Strong

And the Child grew and became strong in spirit, filled with wisdom; and the grace (favor and spiritual blessing) of God was upon Him.

LUKE 2:40 AMP

Grace binds you with far stronger cords than the cords of duty or obligation can bind you. Grace is free, but when once you take it, you are bound forever to the Giver and bound to catch the spirit of the Giver.

E. STANLEY JONES

Lord Jesus, thank You for coming to this earth, taking on human flesh, living among us, and doing Your Father's will. Thank You for the way You lived and what You taught us through Your words and Your example. I pray that my children will grow in the ways that You grew. May they have a sharp focus and clear purpose; may they know why they are here and where they are going; may they have the inner strength to grow strong in character; may they always be about their heavenly Father's business.

Help them to grow, not just in years, but in depth of character and maturity. Give them wholeness in body, soul, and spirit. Bless them with good health, with sound minds, with well-balanced emotions, and may their wills be set on doing all that is pleasing to You. Fill them with wisdom and heap Your grace, favor, and spiritual blessings on them.

Above all, I ask that they will grow strong in spirit—at Your feet, knowing Your worthiness, intimate in their relationship with You, supping and communing with You daily.

Completing a Good Work

I am convinced and sure of this very thing, that He Who began a good work in you will continue until the day of Jesus Christ [right up to the time of His return], developing [that good work] and perfecting and bringing it to full completion in you.

PHILIPPIANS 1:6 AMP

The needed change within us is God's work, not ours. The demand is for an inside job, and only God can work from the inside. We cannot attain or earn this righteousness of the kingdom of God: it is a grace that is given.

RICHARD J. FOSTER

Thank You, Father, that You are a Faithful God and I can put my complete trust in Your trustworthiness. I am so grateful for the way You are working in my life and in the lives of my children. I thank You that the work You are doing is a beautiful work, a good work, a perfect work, full of promise and hope. Thank You, that You do not begin a work within us and then leave it up to us to bring it to maturity and completion.

Develop and deepen my children's trust in You so they will never waver and their faith will continue to grow. May they be confident, convinced, and fully persuaded in their hearts that You will never fail them.

Reassure them that the work You have begun in them will continue and come to completion. Thank You that by Your Holy Spirit, You are making them into all You desire them to be. Breathe into them, Father, Your life; form within them Your image; work within them what is pleasing in Your sight.

Abundant Life

I am the door. If anyone enters by Me, he will be saved, and will go in and out and find pasture.... I have come that they may have life, and that they may have it more abundantly. I am the good shepherd. The good shepherd gives His life for the sheep.

John 10:9–11 NKJV

Jesus Christ opens wide the doors of the treasure house of God's promises, and bids us go in and take with boldness the riches that are ours.

Corrie ten Boom

Lord Jesus, thank You for the door that You have opened for my family and me to enter into the life that is found in You. Thank You for giving Your all so that we can have Your fullness; for shedding Your blood so we can know Your forgiveness; for sending Your Holy Spirit so we can enjoy Your nearness. Thank You for what it means to be saved and to know You; what it means to have You as our Shepherd; what it means "to go in and out" and find pasture; what it means to partake of life that is abundant.

I pray today that my children will know the height, breadth, length, and depth of Your abundant life. May they find the fulfillment of the deepest desires of their hearts. May they understand why they are here and who You made them to be. May they find You to be the answer to every need of life—their need for love, acceptance, purpose, and meaning. May they come to understand that the deepest longing of their heart is Your voice calling them to Your heart.

New Things

Do not [earnestly] remember the former things; neither consider the things of old. Behold, I am doing a new thing! Now it springs forth; do you not perceive and know it and will you not give heed to it? I will even make a way in the wilderness and rivers in the desert.

Isaiah 43:18–19 AMP

The Lord God loves you. He says to you, "Behold, I make all things new. Yes, even you!"

Basilea Schlink

Lord, thank You for what You came to do and for what You are doing in the lives of those who put their trust in You. How wonderful it is to know You have come to make my children new. Thank You for the new things You want to do in their lives—giving them life, bringing them hope, building their faith, conforming them to Your likeness.

Keep their hearts full of expectancy as they reach out for new things of Your kingdom; keep their spiritual life vibrant as they walk down new paths of Your will; keep their vision ever expanding as they climb new heights of Your grace. May nothing about their relationship with You become stale or stagnant, but be always fresh and ever flowing.

May their eyes be fixed on what is ahead and not on the things of the past. May they experience new adventures of seeing You work Your wonders. May new joys and new vision spring forth within them. Make a way for them through every wilderness of life; bring to them Your refreshing rivers; be to them their heart's delight.

Section
7

The Impact of Courage

Be strong, courageous, and firm;
fear not nor be in terror before them, for
it is the Lord your God Who goes with
you; He will not fail you or forsake you.

DEUTERONOMY 31:6 AMP

Courage impacts our lives and the lives of our children in powerful ways. Courage helps us move forward when we would rather turn back, helps us face a problem when we would rather avoid it, helps us resolve a difficulty when we would rather ignore it, helps us to do the right thing when the opportunity is there to compromise, and helps us to overcome rather than retreat or surrender.

A child, when alone, may lack the courage to walk on a pathway that leads through a dark and mysterious forest. However, when the child takes the hand of a parent and walks together on that pathway, courage comes. The courage that our children need to face life and all its difficulties is found in the Lord. Pray that our children will live their lives with assurance of His presence, that He is with them; with confidence of provision, that He will not fail them; and with the reliance on His power, that He is enough.

A Heritage of Strength

"No weapon formed against you shall prosper, and every tongue which rises against you in judgment You shall condemn. This is the heritage of the servants of the LORD, and their righteousness is from Me," says the LORD.

ISAIAH 54:17 NKJV

If you need more strength, you will have it, be sure of that.

PRISCILLA MAURICE

Almighty God, You are the Mighty Warrior. All our strength comes from You who has all power. You are the omnipotent One, the God of majesty, God of truth, God of every victory. Thank You that Your promises can be completely trusted. Your throne is in the heavens, and Your rule and reign is over all. Thank You for Your promise to guard my children against any weapon formed against them.

May my children look to You, trust in You, and lean on Your resources every day and every moment. When facing temptation, make them strong to resist and say "no" to everything that would draw them away from You. Help them to say "yes" to everything that will draw them closer to Your heart. When facing lies, protect their minds with the shield of Your powerful truth. When facing deception, keep their feet on Your pathway of righteousness and peace. When facing false accusations, draw close to them and affirm them in Your all-encompassing, all-embracing love. When facing doubts and fears, help them to raise high their shield of faith and quench all the fiery darts of the Enemy.

Good Courage

Be strong and of good courage, do not fear nor be afraid of them; for the LORD your God, He is the One who goes with you. He will not leave you nor forsake you.... And the LORD, He is the One who goes before you. He will be with you, He will not leave you nor forsake you; do not fear nor be dismayed.

DEUTERONOMY 31:6, 8 NKJV

We walk without fear, full of hope and courage and strength to do His will, waiting for the endless good which He is always giving as fast as He can get us able to take it in.

GEORGE MACDONALD

Lord, I pray that my children will find their strength in Your strength and that they will live victorious lives because You have conquered every foe. May their hands be joined in Yours, touching as You touch; may their feet follow Your footsteps, moving as You move; may their hearts be one with Yours, feeling as You feel; may their wills be one with Your will, working as You work.

I ask that each child be strong and stand tall. As they grow in their walk with You, keep their courage unwavering, their obedience complete, their purpose certain, their lives true. Assure them, Lord, that they never need to walk in fear or doubt, because You go with them, because You will not fail them, and because You will not forsake them.

I thank You, Lord, that You are the mighty God, that You are all powerful, that You are without limitation.

Overcoming the World

You belong to God, my dear children. You have already won a victory over those people, because the Spirit who lives in you is greater than the spirit who lives in the world.

1 JOHN 4:4 NLT

You can fight with confidence where you are sure of victory. With Christ and for Christ victory is certain.

ST. BERNARD OF CLAIRVAUX

I thank You, Jesus, that Your Spirit in my children is greater than anything they will face in this world. You have overcome the world. May they always have a quick response of obedience to You—saying "yes" to Your righteousness and saying "no" to temptation and sin. Keep them and protect them from the Evil One and establish their hearts in Your truth. May they always know that because You live in them, they can live abundantly, purposefully, and victoriously.

Thank You for what Your life, Your death, and Your resurrection have accomplished to transform our lives. Thank You for facing Satan and defeating him; thank You for living in the world and overcoming it; thank You for facing temptation and refusing to yield to it; thank You for tasting death and defeating it.

I pray that my children will see You in Your glory, know You in Your fullness, and live their lives in Your overcoming power. May they know You, not just as their Savior, their Friend, or their Shepherd, but as their very life.

Real Life

But of Him you are in Christ Jesus, who became for us wisdom from God—and righteousness and sanctification and redemption—that, as it is written, "He who glories, let him glory in the LORD."

1 CORINTHIANS 1:30–31 NKJV

The Christian faith is meant to be lived moment by moment. It isn't some broad, general outline—it's a long walk with a real Person.

JONI EARECKSON TADA

Heavenly Father, thank You for Jesus, Your only begotten Son, Your perfect gift who is too wonderful for words! Thank You that Jesus not only lives at Your right hand in heaven, but He also lives within the hearts of those who believe in Him and receive Him.

Thank You for making it possible for my children to know Jesus—personally, truly, intimately, and completely. I ask that they will never live a fake life or pretend life, but the real life You have made possible for them to live. May their hearts fully understand what it means *to believe in* Jesus and also *to be in* Jesus. May they know in reality that Jesus is all they need—their wisdom, their righteousness, their holiness, their purity, their goodness, their redemption, their hope, and their future.

May each child live a life of joyful celebration over their relationship with Jesus. May they be caught up in His beauty, filled up with His love, and taken up with the great commission to make Him known to this generation.

Promises to Trust

For Jesus Christ, the Son of God, does not waver between "Yes" and "No."... As God's ultimate "Yes," he always does what he says. For all of God's promises have been fulfilled in Christ with a resounding "Yes!" And through Christ, our "Amen" (which means "Yes") ascends to God for his glory.

2 Corinthians 1:19–20 nlt

Our feelings do not affect God's facts. They may blow up, like clouds, and cover the eternal things that we do most truly believe. We may not see the shining of the promises—but they still shine! [His strength] is not for one moment less because of our human weakness.

Amy Carmichael

Thank You, Father, that what is written in Your Word has been spoken from Your heart. I am so grateful that Your promises come from the mouth of One who cannot lie. You have not only given my family and me precious promises, but You have guaranteed their fulfillment to us through Your Son, Jesus Christ. Because Jesus is the Truth, Your promises are the truth. Because of Jesus, Your promises are not meaningless, hollow words, but full of life, hope, and power.

Help my children to put their trust and keep their trust in Your promises, no matter what. When they are in need, may they receive the promise of Your provisions; when they are aware of their weaknesses, may they discover the promise of Your strength; when they are troubled, may they know the promise of Your peace; when they are seeking, may they find the promise of Your guidance; and when they know their inadequacy, may they embrace the promise of Your grace.

Section
8

The Power of Purpose

"For I know the plans I have for you,"
says the LORD. "They are plans
for good and not for disaster,
to give you a future and a hope."

JEREMIAH 29:11 NLT

There is great power in the life of someone who has a God-given purpose to fulfill, whose heart is passionate about that purpose, and whose will is set on fulfilling it. The plans of God for our lives should excite us, motivate us, and energize us to seek Him with all our being. His plans are only good, only right, only pure, only the best.

Children need guidance and direction. They need to understand why they are here, where they are going, and how to get there. They need to know that their lives have a God-given purpose that He can fulfill through them. As parents we need to pray that our children will know the plan God has for them, the path they are to follow, the steps they need to take, the direction they need to go, the dangers they need to avoid, the pace they need to travel, and the final destination of their journey.

Strength and Caring

You have taught children and infants to tell of your strength, silencing your enemies and all who oppose you. When I look at the night sky and see the work of your fingers—the moon and the stars you set in place— what are people that you should think about them, mere mortals that you should care for them?

PSALM 8:2–4 NLT

When God has become our shepherd, our refuge, our fortress, then we can reach out to Him in the midst of a broken world and feel at home while still on the way.

HENRI J. M. NOUWEN

I thank You God, Lord of the universe, designer and maker of all that is in the heavens and all that is on the earth, that You are mighty and that You alone do marvelous things. I thank You that You have not only made my children, shaped them, and breathed into them the breath of life, but that You look out for each one. You have taught them from infancy about Your mighty strength, Your awesome power, and Your infinite wisdom.

It is amazing to me to realize, not only how great You are, but how much You care about the lives of my children. You see, know, understand, and care about every detail of their lives. It is in You that they live and move and have their being.

Thank You that my children are on Your mind and in Your thoughts today. I pray that their hearts would trust in You, that their thoughts would turn toward You, and that their feet would follow You all the days of their lives.

The Right Path

Direct your children onto the right path, and when they are older, they will not leave it.

<small>PROVERBS 22:6 NLT</small>

We may not all reach God's ideal for us, but with His help we may move in that direction day by day as we relate every detail of our lives to Him.

<small>CAROL GISH</small>

Father, thank You for Your promise to keep my children on the right path. I pray that they would love Your ways and Your will and carry Your songs of joy in their hearts. May their relationship with You be constant and growing. I pray that they will never depart from what is good, from what is true, or from what is right. May they celebrate the life You have given them, appreciate their uniqueness, and fully embrace the desires You place within their hearts.

I pray for Your direction in my life so that I can bring direction to my children's lives. I need Your training in order to train them up in the way they should go. Give me daily wisdom to speak the right things and do the right things. Place Your words in my mouth and guide my footsteps on Your pathway.

Give my children Your wisdom so that they may have wise guidance; give them Your holy love so that they may choose what is truly best; give them light and understanding so that they may clearly see the pathway to Your will.

No Eye Has Seen

As the Scripture says, What eye has not seen and ear has not heard and has not entered into the heart of man, [all that] God has prepared (made and keeps ready) for those who love Him.... Yet to us God has unveiled and revealed them by and through His Spirit, for the [Holy] Spirit searches diligently, exploring and examining everything, even sounding the profound and bottomless things of God.

1 CORINTHIANS 2:9–10 AMP

As we grow in our capacities to see and enjoy the joys that God has placed in our lives, life becomes a glorious experience of discovering His endless wonders.

WENDY MOORE

Heavenly Father, thank You for the realities of Your Kingdom. Thank You that You have more for us to see, to hear, and to know in our hearts than we have ever imagined. I pray that the realities of Your unseen world will always have a greater influence on the lives of my children than the realities of the physical world that they see, hear, and touch every day.

May they daily see You with spiritual eyes, hear You with spiritual ears, and touch You with the outstretched hand of faith. May Your light fill their vision, may Your touch warm their hearts, may Your voice be the loudest sound they hear within them.

Through Your Holy Spirit, continue to show my children things their eyes have never seen, speak things their ears have never heard, and reveal things their hearts have never known about the wonders You have prepared for them.

Reveal Our Path

The secret things belong unto the Lord our God, but the things which are revealed belong to us and to our children forever, that we may do all of the words of this law.

DEUTERONOMY 29:29 AMP

I believe that nothing that happens to me is meaningless, and that it is good for us all that it should be so.... As I see it, I'm here for some purpose, and I only hope I may fulfill it.

DEITRICH BONHOEFFER

Lord, how wonderful are Your ways, how great is Your understanding, how vast is Your knowledge, how deep is Your love, how wise are Your plans, how mighty is Your strength, how complete is Your salvation, how perfect is Your Word. Thank You that You have revealed to us all that we need to know in order to do Your will and to find Your purpose for our lives.

I pray that my children will be seekers after Your treasures, finders of Your blessings, receivers of Your gifts, discoverers of the riches of Your grace, possessors of Your abundant life, explorers that find the hidden wealth on Your pathways.

Open up to them, Lord, the knowledge that will guide their understanding and the wisdom that will direct their footsteps. Assure them that they will always have enough light to take the next step and to do the next thing. I pray that they will receive all that belongs to them because they are Your children. May their greatest delight be found in the joys of their obedience to You.

Light of the Lord

How precious is Your steadfast love, O God! The children of men take refuge and put their trust under the shadow of Your wings. They relish and feast on the abundance of Your house; and You cause them to drink of the stream of Your pleasures. For with You is the fountain of life; in Your light do we see light.

PSALM 36:7–9 AMP

Nothing can compare to the beauty and greatness of the soul in which our King dwells in His full majesty. No earthly fire can compare with the light of its blazing love.

ST. TERESA OF AVILA

I thank You, Lord, that You are Light and in You there is no darkness, no shadows, no confusion, no lies, no deceit. Thank You that You are the light of the world and the light of life. Thank You that Your light never flickers, grows dim, burns down, or goes out.

I pray that my children will see the splendor of Your light—that its beam will shine on their pathway; that its flame will warm their hearts; that its beauty will lift their spirits; that its glow will shine on their faces.

Send Your light, Lord, to inspire my children, to build their faith, to renew their hope, to strengthen their courage, to lighten their steps, and to encourage them on their spiritual journey. Give them clear direction, make straight paths for their feet, keep them from taking a wrong turn, show them where to place their feet. Give them enough light to take the next step, and lead them to take refuge in You.

A Hope and a Future

The steps of a good man are ordered by the LORD, and He delights in his way. Though he fall, he shall not be utterly cast down; for the LORD upholds him with His hand.

PSALM 37:23–24 NKJV

God's wisdom is always available to help us choose from alternatives we face, and help us to follow His eternal plan for us.

GLORIA GAITHER

Lord, I thank You that You know all things, that You can be fully trusted, that You are completely faithful. Thank You for the wisdom of Your ways and the goodness of Your plans—I know that You have only good things in Your heart for my children. Thank You that they never have to guess or find their own way in life because You will lead them and guide them in the way they should go.

My children's futures are bright because Your light shines on them. Their futures are right because Your will has planned them; victorious because Your might has secured them.

I ask You, Lord, to prosper each child—to make them rich in Your riches, to make them strong in Your strength, to make them blessed with Your blessings. I ask that Your perfect plan for each one will be accomplished as they yield their hearts to You, as they put their trust in You, and as they follow You. Thank You that You are their certain hope and glorious future.

Follow His Way

Blessed is the man who walks not in the counsel of the ungodly...but his delight is in the law of the LORD, and in His law he meditates day and night. He shall be like a tree planted by the rivers of water, that brings forth its fruit in its season, whose leaf also shall not wither; and whatever he does shall prosper.

PSALM 1:1–3 NKJV

We have a Father in heaven who is almighty, who loves His children as He loves His only-begotten Son, and whose very joy and delight it is to succor and help them at all times and under all circumstances.

GEORGE MUELLER

Thank You, Lord, for the blessings that are ours as we listen when You counsel us, follow where You lead, and walk in the way You have prepared for us. I pray that my children's values will be based on what You value and that Your approval will be their greatest delight.

Help my children heed what You say in Your Word, meditate on Your instruction, and listen to what You are saying in their hearts. May all of these things be reflected in their character and behavior.

Bless their lives like a tree that is planted by rivers of water. May their roots go down deep into Your wisdom; may their branches blossom with Your understanding; may their lives bring forth the peaceful fruits of righteousness. I pray that their character will grow strong, grow straight, and grow tall. I thank You that You will nurture and prune them with the hands of a loving vinedresser so that the fruitfulness of their lives will increase and be abundant.

Section 9

The Privilege of Knowing God

This is eternal life, that they may
know You, the only true God,
and Jesus Christ whom You have sent.

JOHN 17:3 NKJV

There is nothing greater in life than knowing God and His Son, Jesus Christ—this is our highest calling, our greatest purpose, our richest treasure, our deepest love, and our fullest joy. Above all, as we pray for our children, we need to pray they will know Him—personally, fully, truly, completely.

What an awesome privilege our children have been given: to know God. This is why they have been created: not just to hear about God, not just to learn about God, not just to read about God, not just to know about God, but to actually know God in reality and in truth. Our children's hearts were made to be filled with Him, to talk with Him, to fellowship with Him, to walk with Him, to worship Him, and to delight in Him. They were made to know what He thinks, feel what He feels, and desire what He desires. This is God's plan—that our children would know and glorify Him.

Answered Prayer

I prayed for this child, and the Lord has granted me what I asked of him. So now I give him to the Lord. For his whole life he will be given over to the Lord.

1 Samuel 1:27–28 niv

I *do not believe that there is such a thing in the history of God's kingdom as a right prayer offered in a right spirit that is forever left unanswered.*

Theodore Cuyler

Heavenly Father, today I affirm anew that the gift You have given to me—my children—I fully give back to You. I place them within Your hands and Your keeping. Continue to give me the wisdom I need to guide their steps on Your pathway and to help them know Your plan and purpose for their whole lives.

Knowing that I can bring to You the prayers of my heart—carrying with them my deepest longings and strongest desires—is a great blessing. You have heard my heart's cry for a family, and You have given me, through my children, more than I could ask or dream. Thank You. What a blessing and joy each one is to me. They help me in so many ways to see and understand Your heart more clearly.

Thank You for Your full, generous, and giving heart. Thank You that You invite them, encourage them, and welcome them to come to You in prayer, to sit at Your banqueting table, to be in Your presence.

Be Known by God

O L**ORD**, *You have searched me and known me.*

P**SALM** 139:1 NKJV

There is no peace like the peace of those whose minds are possessed with full assurance that they have known God, and God has known them, and that this relationship guarantees God's favor to them in life, through death, and on forever.

J. I. P**ACKER**

Lord, I want to thank You for revealing Yourself to us so we can not only know about You, but know You personally. What is even greater, You have told us that we are known by You. I ask that my children will know You fully in their hearts and lives. May they know You in Your holiness, Your beauty, and Your glory. May they know You in Your wonders and in Your ways, in Your power and in Your splendor, and in Your might and in Your majesty.

May they know You personally and intimately. May they look to You as their Father, depend on You as their friend, trust in You as their provider, yield to You as their Lord, and serve You as their King. Above all, may they always be assured that You know all about them. May they rest in the assurance of Your daily care.

Thank You for the privilege of knowing You and being known by You.

Inscribed on His Palms

Can a woman forget her nursing child, and not have compassion on the son of her womb? Surely they may forget, yet I will not forget you. See, I have inscribed you on the palms of My hands.

Isaiah 49:15–16 NKJV

The Lord gives you the experience of enjoying His presence. He touches you, and His touch is so delightful that, more than ever, you are drawn inwardly to Him.

Madame Guyon

Father, it is amazing to me when I realize that Your love for my children is even greater than the love I have for them, that the depth of Your feelings for them goes even deeper than what I hold for them. What a great comfort it is to my heart to know how much You care for them and that they are always in Your thoughts.

May my children always be aware of how much they mean to You, how precious they are in Your sight, how tenderly You carry them in Your thoughts, and that their names are written on the palms of Your gentle hands. Remind them daily, Lord, of Your overwhelming love.

Thank You for being a God of compassion. Help me to remember that You feel deeply and care greatly for my family. Thank You that through Your compassion we can know Your inner feelings toward us, sense Your tender touch upon us, see the riches of what Your heart holds for us, and experience the fullness of what Your love brings to us.

Look to Jesus

We do this by keeping our eyes on Jesus, the champion who initiates and perfects our faith. Because of the joy awaiting him, he endured the cross, disregarding its shame. Now he is seated in the place of honor beside God's throne.

HEBREWS 12:2 NLT

Happiness is found in relationships. And life's greatest happiness is found in life's greatest relationship: a personal relationship with God through Jesus Christ.

KENNETH TANGEN

Thank You, Jesus, that it is all about You—Your work, Your ways, Your glory, Your life, Your love. As I bring my children before You today, my prayer is that they will always—at all times, and in every situation—have You at the very center of who they are and what they do.

May they see You as the One who came for them, died for them, rose for them, ascended for them, and lives for them. May they see You as their High Priest who intercedes for them; as their Shepherd who guides them; as their Friend who cares about them; as their Counselor who speaks to them; as their King who reigns over them.

In all that they do, help them put You in the place that is above all—in their plans, in their choices, in their relationships, in their words, in their attitudes. May Your smile greet them each morning, may Your song be within them each day, and may Your hands of tender mercies tuck them into bed each night.

The Eternal Rock

Open the gates to all who are righteous; allow the faithful to enter. You will keep in perfect peace all who trust in you, all whose thoughts are fixed on you! Trust in the LORD always, for the LORD GOD is the eternal Rock.

ISAIAH 26:2–4 NLT

*Wide as the world is Your command,
vast as eternity Your love;
firm as a rock Your truth shall stand,
when rolling years shall cease to move.*

ISAAC WATTS AND JOHN WESLEY

I am so thankful today, Father, for open gates into Your presence and open arms into Your love. Oh, God, how wonderful You are! You are perfect in every way—without flaw, without error, without stain, without inconsistency, without hypocrisy, without deception, without lies. I am so thankful I can put my complete trust in You.

Keep my children in perfect peace—the peace that only You can give; the peace that passes all understanding; the peace that knows "all is well" because You do all things well; the peace that proclaims with all certainty that "You are in control;" the peace that spreads its wings like the eagle and soars above the storm; the peace of "shalom" that brings Your favor, Your friendship, Your inward rest and tranquility.

Father, bring into my children's hearts all the joys that come from trusting in You, all the strength that comes from leaning on You, and all the delights that come from communing with You, their eternal Rock.

In Unity

Come to Me, all you who labor and are heavy laden, and I will give you rest. Take My yoke upon you and learn from Me, for I am gentle and lowly in heart, and you will find rest for your souls. For My yoke is easy and My burden is light.

MATTHEW 11:28–30 NKJV

The whole reason why we pray is to be united into the vision and contemplation of Him to whom we pray... and with so much sweetness and delight in Him that we cannot pray at all except as He moves us at the time.

JULIAN OF NORWICH

Thank You, Jesus, for calling us, inviting us, and welcoming us to be united with You—joined with You heart to heart, purpose to purpose, will to will, hand to hand, love to love. Thank You for being the balancing point of our lives and for showing us that without You everything gets out of order.

Thank You that You are the God of the light yoke and the easy burden. I pray that my children will know the release, the freedom, and the rest of being yoked to You. Teach them what it means to live with the mind of a servant, to walk with a humble disposition, to respond with a meek spirit, and to reach out to others with a gentle heart.

I pray that they will always trust in Your shed blood to cleanse them from all sin, trust in Your power to lift their burdens, and trust in Your grace to meet the needs of each day.

Divine Helper

I will pray the Father, and He will give you another Helper, that He may abide with you forever—the Spirit of truth, whom the world cannot receive, because it neither sees Him nor knows Him; but you know Him, for He dwells with you and will be in you. I will not leave you orphans; I will come to you.

JOHN 14:16–18 NKJV

Christian hope is applied faith. If God Himself is here with us in His Holy Spirit, then all things are possible.

BRUCE LARSON

Jesus, You are so good to us. Thank You for not leaving us alone, for coming to us, for being with us. Thank You for sending the Holy Spirit, for His presence, for His power, for His companionship, for His comfort. You have promised to not leave us as orphans. Thank You that the Helper, who is exactly like You, has come to abide in us, fill us, and remain with us.

I pray that my children will delight in the sweet fellowship of the Holy Spirit—knowing His voice, having His peace, experiencing His joy. The Holy Spirit has come, not only to be *with* them, but to be *in* them. Help them know the Holy Spirit as their closest, dearest Friend—as the One who encourages them, is always there for them, speaks the truth to them, and genuinely comforts them. Show them that He is their constant helper, He listens to the cry of their hearts, prays for them, cares for them, loves them, and will be with them forever.

Knowing You

But let him who glories glory in this: that he understands and knows Me [personally and practically, directly discerning and recognizing My character], that I am the Lord, Who practices loving-kindness, judgment, and righteousness in the earth, for in these things I delight, says the Lord.

JEREMIAH 9:24 AMP

A vital fringe benefit of being a Christian is the tremendous sense of identity that grows out of knowing Jesus Christ.

DR. JAMES DOBSON

Father, there is nothing greater than to know You. You are greater than all and transcend all there is. Thank You for sending Your only begotten Son to give His life, to shed His blood, and to open the way for us to come into Your presence and know You as our God.

May my children glory in this one thing, that they know You. May their fellowship with You be sweeter and sweeter; may their love for You grow deeper and deeper; may their walk with You become more and more precious; may their knowledge of You increase with every passing year. May they thrive in Your nearness, delight in Your presence, revel in Your goodness, rejoice in Your greatness, and rest in Your love.

May they know You personally, practically, intimately, truly. May they see and know Your heart, may they never forget how much You care about them and care for them. May they recognize Your character and understand Your ways. May they joyously and worshipfully say, "You are my God."

Banner of Salvation

He saved us, through the washing of regeneration and renewing of the Holy Spirit, whom He poured out on us abundantly through Jesus Christ our Savior, that having been justified by His grace we should become heirs according to the hope of eternal life.

Titus 3:5–7 NKJV

Slippings and strayings there will be, no doubt, but the everlasting arms are beneath us; we shall be caught, rescued, restored. This is God's promise; this is how good He is.

J. I. Packer

Thank You, Father, for Your great salvation, so full and free. To not have You is to lose all things, but to have You is to gain all things. Thank You for not only forgiving us for our sins, but also for washing us clean, changing us from within, renewing us by Your Holy Spirit, and assuring us of our hope of heaven.

May "SALVATION" be the banner that flies over the hearts of my children. May its proclamation be on their lips, and its fruit be within their lives. May the joy of their salvation grow greater with each new day. May the hope of heaven always be before them as they go through life, as they make their choices, as they give, and as they serve.

May they never look back, turn back, or be held back as they run their race unhindered; as they keep their eyes on the heavenly prize; as they await their eternal inheritance as joint heirs of Jesus Christ. Help them to make each day count for eternity.

Thank You, Lord,
that You are my children's Provider;
You are their Keeper;
You are their Shepherd;
You are their Healer;
You are their Director.
I place them into Your hands.
I commit them to Your care.
Amen.